FROM OLDHAM

Edited by Lynsey Hawkins

First published in Great Britain in 2000 by
YOUNG WRITERS
Remus House,
Coltsfoot Drive,
Woodston,
Peterborough, PE2 9JX
Telephone (01733) 890066

HB ISBN 0 75431 950 4
SB ISBN 0 75431 951 2

Foreword

This year, the Young Writers' Future Voices competition proudly presents a showcase of the best poetic talent from over 42,000 up-and-coming writers nationwide.

Successful in continuing our aim of promoting writing and creativity in children, our regional anthologies give a vivid insight into the thoughts, emotions and experiences of today's younger generation, displaying their inventive writing in its originality.

The thought, effort, imagination and hard work put into each poem impressed us all and again the task of editing proved challenging due to the quality of entries received, but was nevertheless enjoyable. We hope you are as pleased as we are with the final selection and that you continue to enjoy *Future Voices From Oldham* for many years to come.

Contents

Sidra Jabeen	1
Maxine Williams	2
Dawn Makin	3
Nicola Burns & Millissa Burke	4
Kirsty Whittleworth	5
Daniel Ogden	6
Eleanor Roberts	7
Lauren Worsley	8
Shabnam Kauser	9
Kara Littler	10
Jennifer Carter	11
Daniel Garside	12
Daniel James Grocott	13
Kirstie E Craig	14
Kayley Louise Evans	15
Marc Smith	16
Kerry Samantha Harrison	17
Mark Starr	18
Sam Wood	19
Luke Garnett	20
Amy Mitchell	21
Melanie Ann Clarke	22
Jamie Knox	23
Emma Turner	24
Vikkie Bateman	25
Mark Brocklehurst	26
Abby Wood	27
Mohammed Uzair Rahid	28
Marc Brierley	29
Mohammed Zahid Javed	30
Sara Fielding	31
Stacey Walker	32
Gulshan Maneer	34
Kashif Mahmood	36
Terri Brooksbank	37

Kirsty Riley	38
Danielle Kearsley	39
Jody Taylor	40
Stuart Dickie	41
Suzanne Kinder	42
Sheree Allen	43
Joanne Worsley & Laura Thompson	44
Nicola Starr	45
Adam Rice & David Gauld	46
Natalie Buin	47
Leah Griffiths	48
Emma Deakin & Rachel Cunnane	50
Jonathan Mould	51
Lisa Flynn	52
Fiza Khan	53
Claudine Ollier	54
Richard Atkinson	55
Alison Matthews	56
Leanne Marsland	57
Crystal Bennici & Cheryl Martin	58
Aiden Gilmore	59
Christopher Brown	60
Angela Preston	61
William Murray	62
Ryan Howard	63
Jacqui Bardsley	64
Jenna Higson	65
April Jones	66
Ben Mellor	67
Nicola Ferguson	68
Adam Dockerty	69
Natalie Schofield	70
Stacie Williams	71
Siobahn Oliver	72
Jenna Womersley	73
Kevin Jenkinson	74
Thomas Hibbert	75
Thomas Wibberley	76

Uzma Ghafoor 77
Catherine Kirwan 78
Ryan Price 79
Rebecca Gibbons 80
Jodie English 81
Michelle Previn 82
Carla Connor 83
Shanaz Bibi 84
Saima Kouser 86
Rebecca Bateman 87
Chloe Thomas 88
Diane Warburton 89
Harrison Donegan 90
Leah Critchley 91
Shehzad Ahmed 92
Dale Doherty & Matthew Hayes 93
Paul Hilton 94
Kirsty Tarkenter 95
Chelsea Battersby 96
Danielle Jardine 97
Samantha Harper 98
Melanie Thomas 99
Daniel Stacey 100
Andrew Hurst 101
Dean Barry 102
Sheree Naylor 103
Leigh Robinson 104
Christina Marshall 105
Sean Mooney 106
Martin Kuhnert 107
Shaista Bano 108
Rachel Lomas 110
Nell Cook 111
Resma Khatun 112
Kelly Hadaway 113
Katrina O'Brien 114
Stuart Mills 115
Danielle Tracey 116

Angela Marriott	117
Gemma Buckley	118
Sarah Holbrook	119
Christian Knott	120
Stacey Woodhead	121
Victoria Kenworthy	122
Kerry Kendrick	123
Jiten Panchani	124
Helen Warburton	125
Rebecca Duggan	126
Claire Molden	127
Paul Stevenson	128
Thomas MacNeill	129
Adam Pratt	130
Kirsty Roberts	131
Jenna Sowerby	132
Gemma Gregory	133
Carley Gartland	134
Catherine Barran	135
Claire Marrow	136
Lee T Hughes	137
Sarah Mellor	138
Amanda Seville	139
Vincent Barton	140
Estelle Beckett	141
Emma Kenyon	142
Mark Davenport	143
Simon Baker	144
Rachel Buckley	145
Arron Tierney	146
Hayley Jayne Keight	147
Katy Bailey	148
Kieran Platt	149
Liam Lyons	150
Andrea Peel	151
Nicola Ford	152
Mathew Mosoph	154
Sameena Bibi	155

Barry Woodhouse	156
Robin Garside	157
Claire Dowey	158
Stewart Maxwell	159
Selina Sin	160
Amy Carter	162
Jodie Byrne	163
Jessica Rigby	164

The Poems

LIFE

Ocean of depth
        Others loose interest from life
Downhill process,
        Or glamorous you may say
Is life really a bunch of roses
        Or a sack full of prickly thorns?
Life shines so many lights,
        But which reflects you?

We know life's not always what it seems
It may just be a world of dreams.

Sidra Jabeen (16)

WINTER

W hite, glittery, gleaming snow
I cy, cold, trembling fingertips
N aughty, nasty frost bites
T iny, tingling tiptoes
E ars are bright red
R emeber to wrap up warm.

Maxine Williams (11)

ORANGE FEVER DREAM

Lying in bed I could hear the springs creaking,
I drifted off slowly, my friends were still speaking.
They did not go to sleep
They got in deep.

We had our breakfast
Then had our lessons.
We went to the hall
To have a talk.

Mrs Wood said we could go home
Our parents were on the phone.
We went to pack our bag
Mrs Wood said 'Come back.'

We could not go home
Not everyone was cured
Then I woke up
My friends were still speaking.

Dawn Makin (11)

IN THE CEMETERY

A slimy ghost pushed the cemetery door
Open in the moonlight.
Ooo aaa ooo aaa
A wicked witch cast a spell on me
Ooo aaa ooo aaa.

I was a slimy bat and I turned
Into a vampire.
Ooo aaa ooo aaa
A scary mummy fell into a black
Deep coffin.
Ooo aaa ooo aaa.

A pongy bat flew over the misty
Cemetery
Ooo aaa ooo aaa.

Nicola Burns & Millissa Burke (12)

ORANGE FEVER DREAM

Lying in bed I could hear the springs creaking
I drifted off slowly, my friends were still speaking,
Slowly but surely I fell into a dream.
It wasn't that bad but was not what it seemed.
A school to myself with no one to debate.
On my own, just me, oh wouldn't it be great?

Not a creak from the carpet that my feet were now upon,
A shudder from my spine and an echo from my yawn.

Not a noise in the playground, not a bang, not a sound,
Not a squeak from a mouse and no teachers around.
Just a luxurious palace, not a jail, not a school,
To think it was a prison, you must have been a fool.

But soon I woke up with a bit of a scream,
To find it was just another wish upon dream.

Kirsty Whittleworth (12)

EVIL IAN BRADY

Evil Ian Brady
The beast of the moors
Kidnapped lots of kids
From right under their mum's nose.

In the year England won the cup
He got totally duffed up.
He's taken an overdose once before
Now he's going to Hell's door.

He's killed a couple of kids,
In fact is was five
Later he got arrested
Now he's taken a dive.

He had a companion,
Myra Hindley, she possessed the Devil.
Crimes were committed
And there were several.

Up on the moors,
The bodies that were buried,
Were finally found
And they became worried.

The Jury found them guilty
And then went to jail
Their crime was so bad
They got refused bail.

Daniel Ogden (12)

Jack The Ripper

It was a warm night in August
When he struck his first murder
When he had finished this killing
He went even further.

He slaughtered five women
But altogether murdered eleven
They were all peaceful people
And they went up to Heaven.

He sent the police a letter
Inside it contained a threat
He would chop off his victim's ears
And gradually their death would be met.

He moved very swiftly
That's why he was never caught
Although witnesses swear they have seen him
A cap and long coat he bought.

He walked like a woman
He thought this crime was a game
He thought his life was fairly good
But it would never be the same.

Do not be scared by this story
It happened a long time ago
The murders happened in a quick three months
For his victims it went very slow.

Eleanor Roberts (12)

TRAGIC END TO A NIGHT OUT

We were having a swell night out,
I jumped in my car and drove some friends home.
As I came back I turned the car around
That's when I heard a big pound!

Neil my friend shouted
I shook all over with shock.
I stopped and got out the car door
And to my horror saw Neil on the floor!

'Ring an ambulance' somebody screamed
'Wake up, can you hear me?' someone said,
Blood poured from his head.
What have I done?

Why me? Why now?
I hoped we would spend time together,
But now it's too late,
For you are heading towards Heaven's gate.

I hate myself for what's happened
If only I hadn't been there that day,
I wish I could fly far, far away.
I'll miss you Neil!

Lauren Worsley (12)

He Killed A Girl Now He's In Tears

He's a crying bloke,
But he's a guilty man.
He's looking at the clock,
Waiting, waiting silently to be arrested.
Every second passes, brings more guilty conscience.

I once had the most precious person,
Now he's taken her away.
I don't know what to do,
I might as well kill myself to be with her.

She was pretty like a flower,
She smelled like gladioli
She's smelling the flowers on her grave,
She's scared being in the deep dark ground.

She's screaming for her mummy,
I can hear her screaming.
She's screaming 'Why me?
Why did he kill me I had my whole life in front of me!

Why was I kidnapped by an electrician?
Why did he put me under the floorboards?
Why did I die from asphyxia?
Who can answer these questions?'
'Me' said a crying man.

Then you must be the murderer.

Shabnam Kauser (12)

THE LITTLE ANIMALS

She lived in a town,
The old lady was alone,
She had hundreds of animals and
She never moaned.

Until one day,
Rang the phone,
In her smelly house
She wasn't alone.

The RSPCA came unknown
And one fat lad
With a net and a bag,
The old lady went totally mad.

They took the animals,
One dead kitten
It was so small,
It could fit in a mitten.

She was taken away,
To be sentenced in court
She was sentenced to four years
As she fought.

She loved her animals,
The little kitten was dead
If only they were here,
If only it had been fed.

Kara Littler (12)

The Abused Dog

In Roamstown there was a boy
Who had a dog and abused it so
That it ran away to Landkufor.

It all started one morning
When Billy woke up yawning
He patted the dog, yawned and stretched
Then he got up and played fetch.

He stared at the dog but it did not fetch
Billy said 'Fetch you stupid dog or I'll hit you so
That you won't be able to go out till you're four!'

Billy turned to the dog and raised his hand
His poor little belly got hit by his hand!
He hit him and kicked him till his hand went red
'That will teach you, so now go to bed!'

Mortice walked off, limping bruised and battered
He looked at Billy not in a loving manner
He lay down, looked around and whimpered
He licked his wounds with his tongue.

He scurried to the door and scampered along
Turned to his master and stuck out his tongue!
Ran out of the door and followed the track,
To Landkufor with no slack.

Jennifer Carter (12)

ORANGE FEVER DREAM

Once on a day something occurred
The biggest boom I've ever heard
The Chinese have hit us with a bomb
A bomb of Orange Fever Syndrome.
The disease spread like butter on toast
We were so sick, we put bets on who was sick the most.
Our pens and pencils wrote all day
To our parents' home . . . away.

The school was covered in fences and guards
No one gets in and no one gets out.

The food supply was very short
When I was eating my chips I thought
Looking out of the window,
'When will I get out of this hellhole?'
While everyone was sleeping, I was creeping.

Creeping to knock this snowboarder out,
Heading for the ski slopes.

I knocked him out with one big punch
And then I just took a hunch
That if I could put the boys' clothes on
I could sneak out safe and sound.

Daniel Garside (12)

ORANGE FEVER DREAM

I was lying in bed when I heard a creak,
looked at the door, sprang under my sheet.
Two people entered, tripped over a game,
crashed to the floor, like hailstone or rain.
They got over the pain and got closer singing a tune,
the only way I saw them was by the sparkled moon.

They turned on the light,
I'm in shock, or just fright.
It's my dad and my mum,
waiting for fun.
We crashed down the stairs, raced through the kitchen
but what a pity, can't have fun because my granny is stitching.

Daniel James Grocott (11)

Spook

The picture that hung on the uneven wall
glared down at me and caused me to fall
I ran to the hall through the old oak door
I jumped back with fright could I take anymore?

I ran to the foot of the stairs
Boo hoo hoo!
Where cobwebs entombed me
Boo hoo hoo!

I fled up the stairs to the landing
And there I found a spooky hand
I ran to the nearest door to find
A mirror showing a faraway land.

I touched the old round mirror
Boo hoo hoo!
I felt a river that made me shiver
Boo hoo hoo!

I made my way to the attic
Where I saw the butler covered in static
My hair stood on end and I tried to defend
Myself to the end.

The end
Boo hoo hoo!

Kirstie E Craig (11)

Run Run!

What's that in the dark corner with a pale face?
Run run it's coming *whooo!*
What's that flying across the moon with a loud cackle?
Run run it's coming *whooo!*
What's that rattling of chains upstairs?
Run run it's coming *whooo!*
What's that shiver up my spine?
Run run it's coming *whooo!*
What's that howling on the cliff's edge?
Never mind just run as fast as you can
Zoom!

Kayley Louise Evans (11)

THE GRANVILLE MILL TRAGEDY

One tragic Tuesday
In April '99,
The Granville mill
Burnt in the sunshine

Fire-fighters rushed in
Their hands in a fist
As the huge old mill
Burnt to a crisp

People that were near
Came out of their homes
But all they could hear
Were people's moans

There were children all around
Gazing at the mill
And when the fire had been put out
There was a sudden chill

All you could see were fire-fighters
Wiping away their sweat
After putting out the fire
And the challenges they'd met

But where the old mill
Had once stood
Was now just a heap
Of metal, bricks and charred wood.

Marc Smith (12)

SUNSHINE

Everywhere I go there's sunshine
never rain, never snow, always sunshine
I only dream of sunshine
sunshine gives me power
sunshine gives us life
I love sunshine
and sunshine loves me.

Kerry Samantha Harrison (11)

DISEASE, DISEASE

At school I had a nightmare
I had a bad disease
My friends all called me carrot
It's always me they tease

I was orange on my face
I was orange on my legs
I was orange on my hands
I was orange on my back
I was orange on my toes
I was orange on my nose
I was orange on my neck
I was orange on my arms.

Disease, disease please go away
In a place of no return please stay
Disease, disease just stay away
Let me live longer to play all day.

Mark Starr (11)

ORANGE FEVER DREAM

O ver the past week, orange fever has got on my nerves
R eally really badly
A ll the guards are bugging me
N ever ever stopping
G uards are really horrible because they just stand there looking at you
E ven when you're going to sleep,
they've always got their eyes on you.
F orever I will be here, ever and ever
E ven when I'm older, I'll be still stuck here . . .
V iruses will be spread, all over the world
E veryone will catch it, if they're not careful
R emember orange fever is after you.

Sam Wood (11)

THE HAUNTED HOUSE

A dead looking zombie was getting bitten
by a bloodsucking bat.

Aaagh!

A sharp fanged vampire was sucking
a man's blood.

Aaagh!

A howling werewolf was on
the hill.

Aaagh!

An eight-eyed monster was waiting
under a bed.

Aaagh!

Luke Garnett (11)

Ha, Ha, Ha! Ha, Ha, Ha!

A fat witch
had an itch.

Ha, ha, ha
ha, ha, ha.

See that frog
with a chocolate log.

Ha, ha, ha
ha, ha, ha.

Look at that snake
in a lake.

Ha, ha, ha
ha, ha, ha.

Look at that dragon
with a cannon.

Ha, ha, ha
ha, ha, ha.

Watch out for the clang
it could be a bang.

Amy Mitchell (11)

The Ghost

I saw a spooky shadow on my wall,
I thought they were caving in on me,
I heard a scary sound, *whoooh*
I felt a cold breeze shudder past me,
I got really scared, *whoooh*
My window flew open, I screamed 'Aaahhh,' *whoooh*
I turned around I saw a white glowing sheet, *whoooh*
My mum came in my room, I said I had missed her
She gave me a cuddle!

Melanie Ann Clarke (11)

My Scary Poem

As I walked through the cemetery I heard a noise
Ding, ding, ding, ding, ding, ding, ding, ding,
As I got half way down the cemetery path
Some leaves started to crackle
Ding, ding, ding, ding, ding, ding, ding, ding,
Yellow gloomy eyes watched me
As I walked down the cemetery path
Ding, ding, ding, ding, ding, ding, ding, ding,
Suddenly a zombie started to chase me
Ding, ding, ding, ding, ding, ding, ding, ding,
Wham I shut the cemetery gate
Ding, ding, ding, ding, ding, ding, ding, *ding*.

Jamie Knox (12)

THE SCARY GHOST

I was in my bedroom
The door banged!
I went under my covers
But nothing came.
I came from underneath my covers.

Woooh! Woooh! Woooh!

I saw it!
It was looking straight at me!
It came closer to me
I was getting really scared.

Woooh! Woooh! Woooh!

It said 'I am going to get you.'
I went under my covers but
I still could see it!
Slurp!

Woooh! Woooh! Woooh!

Emma Turner (11)

I WENT TO THE CINEMA NEXT WEEK

I went to the cinema tomorrow,
To see a film next week.
It took one and a half hours
So I didn't watch it,
So I got on the bus
To my house and walked in,
I told my mum I watched it
In a fortnight.

Vikkie Bateman (13)

Nothing At All

Here's a rhyme about nothing at all,
It could be big it could be small.
It has no logic it has no reason,
It could be about any season.
This could be the end of the rhyme,
Or it could be the end of all time.

Mark Brocklehurst (13)

What Nonsense

I got up as I went to sleep
I closed my eyes to take a peep.
I went into the garden to take a bath
And took out the vacuum to clean the path.
I unplugged the telly to watch the news
I went to play darts but couldn't find the snooker cues.
I stood on the table to eat my tea
And closed my eyes so I could see.
I closed the door so I could walk through
And held my hand out to put on my shoe.

Abby Wood (12)

DAVID AND GOLIATH

There was a man called Goliath
He had long hair
And loved to sit in a bath
He was white as a snowflake
He was tall as a giraffe's face
And he lived behind a lake.

He was bad as a silly rat
And sat on people's hats.
He broke the windows
He kicked the doors
He bossed people around
But no one talked to him and made a sound.

There was a boy called David
He was poor
But Goliath always wanted more and more money
David was clever as a tiger catching a deer
And Goliath was dumb as a silly cow.

David didn't like Goliath
So he wanted to solve this.
Goliath was stealing money from the bank
And David hit a catapult
And there was he dead
With a catapult on his forehead.

Mohammed Uzair Rahid

KING ARTHUR AND THE ROUND TABLE

There was a man called Arthur,
He was the king of many knights,
He had a wife called Martha,
They marked their land
And fought for rights.

Arthur had a former partner
Who betrayed him,
His clothes smelt bad, like a dustbin.

They had to fight the last battle
As they got there by cattle,
They fought the knights and slaves
And they lived their lives in caves,
They stabbed and punched the slaves and knights
But then they risked their own lives.

At the end of the battle
Arthur had been killed
But so had his partner the one that smelt.

Before he died he asked Martha
To push his body down the lake
And that's the end of old King Arthur.

Marc Brierley

David And Goliath

This is the myth
Of David and Goliath
Most of the time he was a laugh
But when he was fighting
He was always shivering.

He had black hair
And looked like a bear
Goliath was tall but
David was small.

David was poor
But Goliath wanted more
And more money
And Goliath always was cruel and silly.

One day David came to town
But no one would pay
David made his way by crawling
But Goliath said he was crying.

They started in a headlock
But David got out of the headlock
And got a catapult
And hit him with a catapult!

Mohammed Zahid Javed (12)

MEDUSA

Medusa was a maiden fair,
Who always primped and pampered her hair.
She annoyed a god, I forget his name
And Medusa a vile monster became.

It happened on an island called Seriphus,
Where a young boy was sent, his name was Perseus.
He was found by a fisherman,
Who looked after him till he was a good strong man.

This young boy Perseus is now much older,
He seems to be a lot bolder.
He went to fight the monster Medusa,
All for the sake of the people's producer.

He went to the cave,
It looked like a grave,
Bodies everywhere all turned to stone.
Then from the dark he heard a groan!

He crept into her cave without detection,
He used his shield to see her reflection.
He spotted her there
And took lots of care
He crept further and further forward.

Perseus chopped off her head
With one mighty blow.
Then as he looked he said
'Gosh what an ugly crone.'

He picked up her head
And went back through the cave,
That he said looked very much like a grave.
He went back to the house of Minerva and there,
She fixed it to her cape of fur.

Sara Fielding (13)

MOSES OF THE BULRUSHES

There was a boy called Moses
Who was left in reeds and roses
One day an Egyptian princess came
And rescued him from death and pain
Now Moses is a lucky boy
For he could have been destroyed.

She taught him all his rights and wrongs
For when he grew up to be big and strong
She loved and cared for him so very dear
So now she keeps him close and near.
She tried to hide him from the Pharaoh
Because he was very mean
He wanted to kill all the baby boys
And Moses could have been destroyed.

She brought him up as her own
One day she hoped he'd get the throne.
As Pharaoh went to look for boys
She tried to hide Moses' noise
She gave him a drink
She gave him some food
But Moses just wanted to laugh and play.

When Moses grew up to be big and strong
He killed an Egyptian, he knew it was wrong.
One day he saw two men fighting in the wood
He tried to stop them, but they just said
'Don't stop us you killed an Egyptian'
And then Moses understood.

If the Pharaoh heard of Moses
He would kill him in reeds and roses
Moses left to live in Midian
There he pretended to be an Egyptian
Because it would be safer.

Stacey Walker (12)

NOAH'S ARK

There was a wise man named Noah,
He had hair down to the floor,
He would do anything he could
But he would stop and think if he should,
You would describe him as quite handsome
But you wouldn't say he was dumb,
He had a long, dark, soft beard,
In his life was someone he feared.

One day Noah built a big boat,
He hoped that it would float,
The boat was about three floors tall,
Each floor as big as a school hall,
On it were different creatures,
They all had different features,
On it were lots of animals,
Like lions, tigers and goats,
But they all used their brains
And never fought.

Noah brought on the boat
Animals of all kinds,
But he would not be cruel to them
If they were blind,
Some animals were very small,
But Noah never treated them like a ball.

One day the heavy rain finally came,
Noah was so scared he forgot his name,
The heavy rain went on into a flood,
Like three thousand buckets of blood.
The rain went higher than the mountains
It was like a big massive fountain.

One day the rain stopped,
It was like someone had mopped
And Noah and all the animals
Lived happily ever after.

Gulshan Maneer (13)

My Brilliant Poem

There was a woman who was a postman
She was a normal woman and didn't have a name.
She went downstairs to the roof
She was busy but had nothing to do
So went upstairs to the basement
She switched off the TV
She went outside and started vacuuming the ceiling.
She felt tired so she went to sleep for one minute
And woke up two hours later.
It was night but the sun was shining
And she started delivering letters
She did this every day
What a normal person don't you agree?

Kashif Mahmood (12)

Brain Drain

My eyes are wide open
My mind is blank
Are these wires controlling my mind?

I feel like a laboratory rat
Waiting for the experiments to begin
Are these wires controlling my mind?

They sit there with a clipboard
Taking down notes
I feel so much pain
Are these wires controlling my mind?

Terri Brooksbank (14)

Why?

Why is it me who sits on the floor?
Why is it me who can't learn anymore?
The pain I have
The pain I feel
Why is it me?

We have done no wrong
My baby and I
Why should we starve?
Why should we die?
My baby can't cry he is too weak
Death is upon us
We will not survive.

Kirsty Riley (13)

EVERY PICTURE TELLS A STORY

I can't believe this is happening to me
Sitting on the floor in agony
My baby and I
Have done nothing wrong
So why is this happening to me?

I can't feed my baby
I have no food
I don't want my life
To end like this
So why is this happening to me?

Danielle Kearsley (13)

We Need Help!

I need help and support
for my child and me,
we have nothing to eat
and no clothes to wear,
we need help!

We have been deserted
we don't deserve it
my child and I will die soon
we need help!

I am suffering in loneliness
in this dull, gloomy room.
We need protection from disease
we need help!

My child needs education
and warmth from the cold.
Is it all my fault? What have I done?
We need help!

I feel helpless and alone
in this cold cruel world
why will no one help us?
They have money and support!
I have nothing, please help us!
We need help!

Jody Taylor (13)

EVERY PICTURE TELLS A STORY

As I climb up the crumbling sandstone rocks,
My hands are shaking out of control,
More and more rocks are falling,
A thousand feet to the ground.

My short hair is lifted lightly,
The wind whispers,
I look upon the endless mountains,
So big, so beautiful.

As I approach the top of the mountain,
I see my ropes falling away,
Now getting back is impossible,
Now the only way is up.

As I sit silently waiting,
Maybe waiting for nothing,
Was that the sound of an aeroplane?
Is rescue close at hand?

A helicopter skims the mountains,
Is it a coincidence?
Is it a miracle?
I stand at the summit and wave.

Stuart Dickie (13)

Do People Care?

Here I am looking for work
No one really wants me
There isn't a single job to spare
But why should people care?

Here I am at home
All alone in my room
I am just sitting there
Does anyone seem to care?

Here I am in bed
On the cold floor
My clothes with every rip and tear
Are you sure that people care?

Here I am shrivelled up
Ill and dying for food
To have any comfort is very rare
I wish there was someone to care!

Suzanne Kinder (13)

My Children

I look down at the other children
With nice neat clothes
I look down at my child
So thin, with no clothes.

I walk around in rags
Trying to buy food
With my baby in my arms
I cry quietly but he is too weak.

At the end of the day
My baby cries with hunger
I feel so angry
I want to run away.

I wake up the next morning
My husband by my side
He goes to seek work
I go to the hospital.

I wait there
Patiently
It's my turn next
I knew it, it's true
Another child is coming.

Sheree Allen (13)

Broken Smile

Now you see a smile on my face,
But soon my face turns bleak,
Thinking back to '22
My memory is all too clear.

I was twelve that day
When they broke into our friendly mud house village
They wrecked our lives
Overpowered us
The men were slaughtered like animals
The women raped and taken to camp.

My face turns bleak, my face turns bleak.

I was told to stand against a wall whilst all my friends were shot,
I was one of the lucky ones
Who were used as slaves
We were made to feel like strangers in our homeland.

My face turns bleak, my face turns bleak.

I can still see the deadly smile the master gave that day
I refused to work
I was in too much pain from beatings
He shut me in a store cupboard for three days
No food, no water
It felt like years.

My face turns bleak, my face turns bleak.

Joanne Worsley & Laura Thompson (14)

Brain Strain

I sit in this chair
a blank expression upon my face
red wires, white wires
clinging to my head.

I wonder what they're doing
as they sit smirking at me
red wires, white wires
clinging to my head.

I'm tied into a chair
I feel so tired and drowsy
red wires, white wires
clinging to my body.

I feel a sharp pain through
my whole body
my eyes begin to flicker and close
red wires, white wires
clinging everywhere.

Nicola Starr (13)

The Quake

I ran from the house with fear in my heart,
As the tremors began to grow stronger.
I stopped in my tracks as rubble fell around me.
Everything went black, I was conscious no more.

I awoke from my slumber to find it was day,
And I knew I was buried under rubble and rock.
A rock moved away and a face way above me
Said in a soft soothing voice help was at hand.

A rope slithered down, he said 'Grab hold.'
This was when I knew I would make it.
I was pulled from my deep and rocky grave.
The heavens opened and rain started to fall,
But that didn't matter because I was free.

Adam Rice & David Gauld (13)

EVERY PICTURE TELLS A STORY

Here I sit
On my own
Outside the mud hut
We call home.

Here I sit
With an empty bowl
And I look across
This barren land.

Here I sit
And I wonder why?
As I stare up
At the burning sky.

Help me, God
I gently cry.

Natalie Buin (13)

TRAPPED

Trapped
Can't feel my body
So cold
Lumps of timber and stone crush me.
How long have I been here?
The days and nights merge together.

But wait! What's that?
Is that a light?
I can't tell
Do I hear voices?
I think I hear voices
I try to move.

A block of stone gives way
The snow turns red
The pain is unbearable
I scream
They hear me
Endeavour to help me
The pain in my leg grows
I couldn't feel my leg before
They shift the wood from my face.

The pain explodes
It sweeps through my body like a tidal wave
I scream again

Suddenly I see a face
I hear a voice
A hand reaches to help me
I say I can't move
I say lumps of wood and stone are crushing me
They say they'll help me
They say I'll survive
I'll survive.

Leah Griffiths (13)

THE CRY FOR HELP

I miss you Mum
Please come back and take me away.
I can't live here
Without you
My only friend is Bobby the sheep
But he is getting old
And soon Daddy will kill him.

Daddy has been touching me
Hurting me
If I cry he hits me harder.

Last night he got very angry
Because I fell asleep
He started hitting me
I couldn't stand it anymore
I had to run away.

Please forgive me . . .

Emma Deakin & Rachel Cunnane (13)

BUTTERFLY

Butterfly
Light as a feather
Bright as the sun
Quiet as a flower in the sun
Gentle as a towel, fresh from the wash.

I see the butterfly in the field
Collecting its pollen
From the red flowers
Blood-red in the green field.

Jonathan Mould (11)

A Cat With A Rocket Pack

There was a cat with a rocket pack
he went and saved his girlfriend
she thought he was a big fat hunk,
when he went to see her she was all tied up
and he got his rocket pack and saved her,
she is called Fizzy and he is called Wizzy.
They went out on a date
and he asked her to marry him.
she said 'Yes' and she
shouted it out so everyone could hear.
He said 'I love you,' and
she said 'I love you too.'

Lisa Flynn (11)

Bats

They're grey and black
There is nothing they lack,
Their eyes are beads
No one knows what they need.

They scream and screech
And to silence they preach
Their ears twitch and flap
When they hear a rat.

There is no place where they can't reach,
Their feet go *screech, screech, screech.*
They suck the blood right out of you
They suck so much that you go blue.

They hang upside down like a trapeze on a rope,
And at the night sky they gawp.
As soon as night strikes
From their silence they break.

Their screech, screech, screech
Breaks up your sleep,
And their flutter flutter flutter
Is as nerve-racking as a nutter.

They're wreckers and noisy
They are very determined.
They are stupid and blind
They are very bad vermin.

Fiza Khan (13)

RAT!

There once was a giant rat,
Who nearly got eaten by a cat,
I wish the cat had swallowed him whole,
Or even scooped him out of a bowl.

If I had a machine gun,
I swear I'd make the rat run,
But even though I don't have one,
I could just pretend I did have one.

When I am older and bigger,
I'll buy a gun and pull the trigger,
I'll shoot the rat,
And make it splat,
Then that will be the end of that.

Claudine Ollier (12)

Me!

I sat with my pen and thought a bit,
and then I thought some more,
'Shall I write about daffodils?'
No, that's been done before!
'Shall I write a mile long epic?
About soldiers or knights of yore?
Not really, silly me, I've already been told,
Thirty lines, no more!'

I sat and thought, 'Such hard work!
A subject I must find,
no matter how I rack my brains,
nothing comes to mind.
What is there no one else has done?
Forget it, I'll watch TV,
I can't relax it's on my mind,
back to the table for my tea!'

At last a thought hit my brain
as I sat and drank my tea
a reflection staring at my eyes
of course, my cup, it's me.
The subject of my poem
as so far you will agree
is my attempt to write these words,
this poem was about *me!*

Richard Atkinson (11)

SCHOOL LIFE

Can't parents see it's not fit for
Consumption?
Can't they see it's something I hate
And are they not nonplussed by my
Look of disgust
And the way I back off from the gate?

What I'd give for a day off school
To skip lessons
Skive off
To hang around and play it cool.

Syril next door who's seven
Sometimes skips to school, oh heaven
And goes for a holiday
Down in Devon.

Alison Matthews (12)

THE SPOOKY SOUNDS

Lying in my bed I could hear the springs creaking
It scared my mouse, it started squeaking.
I was dreaming nicely when something went *boom!*
I suddenly woke up and ran out the room.
I looked outside when I heard a shatter
It was next door's window, my what a clatter.

I sat back on my bed eating *munch, munch, munch.*
And I carried on going *crunch, crunch, crunch.*
I was bursting right to the top
All of a sudden something went *pop!*
And then I woke up all covered in sweat
I suddenly woke up and found it was the worst dream yet.

But the fever's still with me, it won't go away
I sat up and was orange for a day
My friends said 'What a horrible look'
They can't talk, they smell of muck
The fever's gone, it's gone for good
I'm back to normal the way I should.

Leanne Marsland (11)

Every Picture Tells A Story

No mummy, no daddy, nobody to turn to
I run for freedom
The faster I run the faster it follows
My nightmare has just begun
Nowhere to run nowhere to hide from Death.

No mummy, no daddy, no friends, no family
All dead.
Feet numb with pain, heart bleeds with sorrow
Eyes sting with salt tears
My life drains from my body.

No mummy, no daddy, no feeling inside me,
Death fills the empty space.
No point in running,
It will catch up with me soon
No pain, no suffering, but no more life
Will it be the death of freedom?

No mummy, no daddy, no me
I huddle and wait
Wait for it to come and take my empty shell
Under a sheltering bush
Thorns stick in my side
I wait for Death.

Crystal Bennici & Cheryl Martin (13)

THOUGHTS

I look upon my dusky city
think many thoughts
some thoughts of pity
some thoughts are happy
and others sad
but I know I'm not doing bad.

I have regrets
regrets I hate
I regret this job
and I'm only eight.

If I don't work
my family will pay
they will suffer bad
in a terrible way.

We'll have no drink
no clothes, no food
we'll have to travel
round all nude.

Aiden Gilmore (13)

Bat Attack

Screech, screech, here come the bats
their silky wings silhouette the ground
in the milky moonlit sky as
they go to attack the town of Wigan
also known as the land of pies.

Their hairy bodies, their massive ears
and their dark complexions complete
the hideous figure,
but these bats are no ordinary bats,
they are three feet, five inches in height
with razor-sharp teeth,
nasty eyes with a real nasty grin.

These bats originate from Dracula's lair,
their bloodthirsty thoughts send
a shiver down one's spine,
but once put in sunlight, they, by magic,
fizz, melt and disappear without a trace.
But whilst fizzing away, they make more
and more until the town of Wigan
has been overrun and wiped out.
They move on to destroy another city,
town, village or hamlet. *Ha, ha, ha!*

Christopher Brown (13)

Squirrels!

We are bushy-tailed squirrels
and we squeak, squeak, squeak
but on some strange occasions
we speak!

We run around and attack animals
we are nasty and vicious
and we find it delicious
we have no friends in this town
and it's bringing us down
But this doesn't mean we can't have
Fun!

We don't like people, they're big and smelly
and they have big bellies like bowls of jelly.
They think they can kill us an
make us extinct
but *ha!* That's what they think.

Angela Preston (12)

INSECT FRENZY

I saw some insects coming down the street
Millions and millions like an army fleet.
Ants, beetles and lots, lots more
Just millions crawling across the floor
Some small and hairy
Just a little scary
Tip, tap was all you heard
But to be honest nobody cared.

I saw some insects coming down the street
Millions and millions like an army fleet
The ants, the beetles and the rest
All coming together thinking they were the best
Some big, some small
Some just can't wait, owning the mall
They all set off to conquer the town
But when they lost they all pulled a sad frown.

William Murray (12)

UNTITLED

The mice came, they were under the floorboards
In the kitchen
doing some pinching
they were down in the sofa
under the chairs
eating all the apples and pears.

They smell and squeak
they're really unique
we were all very scared
and we all heard a little bird
chewing on a little mouse
and blood dripping, almost like it was coming out of a spout.

Ryan Howard (12)

A Vermin Poem

All day long the squirrel
sleeps. Then all night
the squirrel eats.

They run and scatter
and make a clatter.
The noise they make
for goodness' sake,
'Shut up you stupid squirrels.'

Squirrels are vermin.
They pinch your food,
they are so rude.

Jacqui Bardsley (12)

THE PLAGUE OF VAMPIRE BATS

A quaint old village was Howarth.
It was very small.
This is where my ditty begins.
The vampire bats invaded Howarth
They came with so much power
And all they ate was chicken and carrots.

The bats ate rats as fat as cats
The screeched and squealed and ate big meals.
And when they got angry
They ate all things banging
And once they ate the wrong thing
And died of a bad attack.

Jenna Higson (12)

Whisper, Whisper

Whisper, whisper, whisper goes my sister down the phone.
Whisper, whisper, go the branches as they blow in the wind alone.
Whisper, whisper, whisper sleeps the river on the story.
Whisper, whisper go my parents, whisper on and on.
Whisper, whisper, whisper, whisper, I so mind
The whisper, whisper, whisper, it is tiring but sometimes
I wish the whispering would shut up nice!

April Jones (11)

I Miss

I miss Thomas,
I miss going to the shop,
I miss primary school.
I miss my old friends,
I miss my sister Amieé
I miss my old teachers.

Ben Mellor (11)

TEENAGER HIT BY FRIEND'S CAR DIES

It was just after midnight
October the fourth
When Neal Stephan Tombs
Was killed with such force.

It was 4.50am
When Neal died
I cried and cried
I was hurt inside.

We had some good laughs
Neal and the lads.
He was one of the best
Now he's at rest.

I'll have to live every day
With the guilt I feel
The hurt will never go away
I'll never forget you, Neal.

Nicola Ferguson (12)

TRAIN TRAGEDY

Early this morning,
Twenty-six people died,
As a train switched tracks,
Which caused them to collide.

The train to London,
At seventy miles per hour,
Hit the other train,
With terrific power.

The slow train to Wiltshire,
May have caused the crash,
As it switched tracks,
Took a great bash.

The people on the trains,
To work they hurried,
Not knowing that they were,
To be dead and buried.

Many people helped,
Helped and tried,
To dig out the bodies,
Of those who had died.

We will never know,
How many lost their lives,
But we do know,
Many more survived.

Adam Dockerty (12)

PADDINGTON'S DISASTER

Yesterday in London,
a tragedy occurred,
there was a great train crash,
and everything went blurred.

The people panicked,
and children cried,
when the train crashed,
people died.

Brothers and sisters,
people of all ages,
got killed in the crash,
couldn't collect their wages.

They could never see their families,
ever again,
because of one train,
with no clockwork brain.

It went through a red light,
and went straight through the other train,
everything set alight,
people burnt alive and writhed in pain.

And so I have told this story,
of what happened two years ago,
they never bothered to fix it,
I think their standards are quite low.

Natalie Schofield (12)

THE MAN WITH A FAKE NAME!

Two months ago
There was a man in Liverpool
He passed himself off as a piano teacher
And decided to play it cool.

He taught two girls
Who loved him dearly
He harassed them both
And then they saw it clearly.

One of the girls killed herself
The other one made a statement
The police questioned him
But he kept them patient.

The man pleaded innocent
And lied to the police
The girl decided not to press charges
And he ran away on his release.

The fake piano teacher
Turned out to be the one they were looking for
They were so annoyed
But they could do nothing more.

They found the fake man's name
To find him they fled
But didn't succeed
The real name belonged to a man who was dead.

So next time beware
In case you meet a man with a fake name
Cos the man you meet could be
Totally *insane!*

Stacie Williams (12)

TEENAGER HIT BY FRIEND'S CAR DIES

It was just after midnight
on October the fourth
when Neal Tomb was killed
by a car with such force.

He was taken to hospital,
but died on the way
and the driver was treated for shock.
Mark Hewitt was driving some friends home
after a night in Grasscroft.

Neal was a much loved lad
he was as former pupil at Saddleworth School.
Everyone adored him
he was very quiet, smashing but cool.

Now Neal has lost his life
any information would be nice
before you want to take your car
please think twice.

Siobahn Oliver (13)

GOLDEN

After fifty years I can't stop dancing,
It's been fifty years long, golden I say
We danced the night away.
We met dancing and still do,
As anyone being together for this long would.

We are intergrable from dance
If I carry on I might go into a trance.
Our family are wonderful, they support us so much,
They say we're as good as professionals in a book.

It started at Mump's bus garage then Penine lounge,
They do sequence dance sessions at St Barnabas' Church hall
just for us.

We do bowling as well as dance,
So I don't think I will go into a trance.
I worked as a warden for pensioners before I retired.
I'm glad I did or I would be tired.

Jenna Womersley (12)

A TEENAGER'S TRAGEDY

What a tragic waste of life
Family and friends are so sad
His life snuffed away like a candle
Ever so young, he who was just a lad.

Then he was hit by a car
It happened in a blink
He was in the middle of the road
So I didn't have time to think.

When I realised what I'd done
I was just so scared
I got out of my car
But all I did was stare.

It was a tragic end to a night out
He was such a smashing lad
Family and friends will miss him
All of them will be sad.

Kevin Jenkinson (12)

Jack The Ripper

In 1888 it wasn't safe,
Jack the Ripper took his place,
The women worried,
The men scurried.

Hooker by hooker,
Jack the Ripper.
He bit like a nipper,
Better watch out
Jack's about.

Sledgehammer on the
Back of the head,
He'll put you in
A hospital bed,
He stabs you slow,
The blood starts to flow.

In King's army court
He confessed to murder,
The people started booing,
The judge said 'Order'.

So now today,
Jack's locked away,
And there to stay.

Thomas Hibbert (12)

A Boy With A Dream

Twenty years ago
a little skinny lad,
he fell in love with football,
and that was all he had.

He got rejected by Arsenal
and other clubs as well,
I was down a bit today,
so then I said, 'Oh well!'

Then my luck struck again
'cause I was picked for Man United
I just couldn't believe it,
and I was so excited.

In a week's time I would play my first match,
I hope I score a goal,
or at least have a shot.
or I'll be back burning coal.

I was in the Theatre of Dreams
playing alongside Giggs and co,
what a great feeling,
who could ask for more?

The day I was picked for England,
I was so proud that it hurt,
my dream had come true,
to wear the three lions on my shirt.

Thomas Wibberley (12)

The Earthquake

In 1884 it began,
There was the earthquake.
The people were horrified,
That they fell into the lake.

First of all nothing fell,
The people were in shock.
But then when everything fell,
The people ran into their flock.

The things fell down,
The room was shaking.
The children were crying,
The noise was faking.

But the people ran away,
On the second floor,
They couldn't get out,
The earthquake rapped the door.

When all the noise had stopped,
They were all outside.
Except poor little Samantha,
Who was left inside.

Everybody was hugging each other,
Fresh air beneath their feet,
They found Samantha,
She was fast asleep.

Samantha's parents went upstairs,
And tugged her away,
They told her about
That horrible day.

Uzma Ghafoor (12)

PAUL

Paul was bright yellow
in the summer morning
Paul was always on the beach
playing in the summer breeze
Paul was a pair of shorts
lying on his own small bed
Paul was a fighting Power Ranger
a piece of chocolate melting
as it slowly disappears.
Paul was a running golden retriever
running in the cool summer winds.
Paul was a spinning tennis ball
that always went the furthest.
Paul was a speeding sports car
the first to be stopped
Paul will always be the golden
sunshine in the morning.

Catherine Kirwan (12)

Christmas Night

It is a freezing cold Christmas night
And outside the streets are lit up bright
The ice lying on the ground
With every step you take comes a cracking sound.

Everybody is having a great time
And everything is absolutely fine
Children's faces full of glee
Opening presents under the Christmas tree.

Toys and games for girls and boys
The room filled with a joyful noise
Time for bed, the happy day is done
'Thank you Dad and thank you Mum.'

Ryan Price (12)

THE MYSTERY DEATH OF VICKY

Pink and white roses
he lay on the ground
by the ditch
where the body was found.

There was a card
that read
'Forever in our thoughts'
simply signed by Mum and Dad.

Gemma Algar was her friend
they went to the Bombay Nite
for her 18th birthday
then she disappeared that night.

Posters for her missing clothes
were pinned up on the wall
with the police number on it
so people can give them a call.

The mystery is,
she has no bruises
and her murderer
just cruises.

Rebecca Gibbons (12)

BLOOD SPORTS

Bears are nasty animals,
they'll chase you till you die,
If I was a person being chased
instead of saying 'Hello'
I would say 'bye bye.'
I'll run till I drop
and hope the bear will stop.
I'll run away,
where can I go?
The bear will catch me
and take me to his home.
Oh no - it's got me
What shall I do?
Phew! What a relief
It's only Baloo!

Jodie English

A Poem About Blood Sports

Today I thought about fox hunting,
And feeling for that little thing,
I've dreamed and dreamed it will be banned,
But no one will put in a helping hand.
The fox is cute and fluffy you see,
But why won't people let it be?
Tony Blair does nothing at all,
'Cause all he does is shouts and bawls.
Foxes like to have a life,
Not to be chopped and slashed with a knife,
People say it's good fun,
Anyway they say what's done is done.

Foxes like to stroll around,
Not to be eaten by a hound,
Foxes like to look for prey,
Not to be buried in a field all day.
Foxes eat chickens and cocks,
Not to have their eyes hidden in socks.
There is one thing I need to know,
What do we do with the poor fox's body?
See, I don't even think they know.

See they say they are having fun,
But again, what's done is done.

Michelle Previn (13)

PLEASE DON'T KILL ME!

I am running through the woods,
I can hear the whistles being blown,
The dogs are barking really loud,
I cannot go much further,
I am feeling dizzy, going to fall down,
Quick, round this corner,
There should be somewhere to hide,
Oh no, I've been blocked off,
Goodbye, my life, goodbye.

Carla Connor (13)

LIVING ALONE - US COCKS

Living alone with nothing to do
pecking on beans, that's all we do.

Being lifted by our feet
in rain and sleet.

Being thrown in a pit
nearly having a fit.

Never know what's coming
maybe life or death.

Being loaded with metals
it was all like hell.

Coming face to face
with a different race.

Never been here,
never been seen.

Tell me why
tell me why so mean.

Living alone with a
life like hell.

Rather be alone
somewhere down a well.

Sitting alone with
nothing to greet.

Life's like this but
not very neat.

Cut and grazed
with all those blades.

Don't know where to go
just kill me and go.

It's all so bright
and it's all just lit.

My life's a living hell
I'm here to tell.

I'm gonna die.
I'm gonna die.
I'm gonna die.

Shanaz Bibi (14)

WHAT IF?

What if they catch me?
What if they don't?
What do I do?
I don't know.

What if they shoot me?
What if they don't?
What will I do with no family at all?

They shot me,
I'm bleeding to death
I'm on the floor
With blood everywhere.

They shot me again
They carried me away.
They got my fur
And now I'm dead!

Saima Kouser (13)

THE PIED PIPER OF HAMELIN

Rats! There were thousands of them,
Probably even more than a thousand and ten.
But there stood tall one queer man,
In two seconds flat we all became a fan.
'Help, help!' we cried 'we will obey.
We'll give you anything, anything to pay.'
Then the mayor offered one bag of gold,
At least that's what I've been told.

'Twinkle dee,
A, B, C,'
That's what the piper piped.
Scuffle, scuffle, scratch, scratch,
Out came not just one rat.
One by one they followed the piper of Hamelin.
'Hip hip hooray the rats are dead,'
'But the mayor has gone back on his word,'he said.
'You shall pay,
For you haven't kept your promise today.'

Once again he played his tune,
Children followed to the place of doom,
All except one, Tiny Tim!
He hopped back,
Down the track,
To tell everyone the sad news.

Rebecca Bateman (12)

Maude Bentley

I was coming home from hospital
And everything was going fine
Then someone came and took my bag
I was angry it was mine.

He punched me and pushed me
Until I was very sore
The next thing I knew
I was on the floor.

I was covered in bruises from top to bottom
My face was like a bruised plum
People say it's a nasty tragedy
And I think that man's dumb.

I am getting all the help I can
People are giving me attention
And people are still searching
For that nasty man.

Chloe Thomas (12)

Neil Tombs

I was waiting for a lift
From a very good friend of mine
I was waiting on Oldham Road
Where everything was going fine.

I was just about to walk
And then I was on the floor
The last thing that I heard
Was the slam of a car door.

I woke up in a hospital bed
With all my friends around me
The doctor walked in and said
What was the last thing you did see?

The last thing that I saw
Was a tiny blade of grass.
Then I woke up here
With a drink of water in a glass.

Diane Warburton

The Undertaker

A cold and stormy darkness
Ooo aaa ooo aaa
Moons
And settles wide and still
And owl amid these shadowy walls
Over a jumble of tumbled stones
Dark on a darker hill.
Grey against grey of ruins
And brittle weeds
Calls and
Soundless swoops away.
Bursting over scattered stones
Pounces
Hovers and sways
Drifting amongst their own bones
Like the webs of the Milky Way.

Harrison Donegan (12)

HAUNTED HOUSE

There was a girl who saw a deadly ghost!
Ooo aaa ooo aaa
She went as white as a ghost
Ooo aaa ooo aaa
She went into a church
Ooo aaa ooo aaa
She saw a spider
Ooo aaa ooo aaa
The girl walked up the creaky stairs
Ooo aaa ooo aaa
She saw a rat
Ooo aaa ooo aaa
She saw a vampire
The vampire said 'Boo!'
Ooo aaa.

Leah Critchley (12)

Ghost House

A zombie walked across the room
Ooo aaa ooo aaa
A ghost came through the wall
Ooo aaa ooo aaa
I heard a goblin in the basement
Ooo aaa ooo aaa
I saw a vampire coming out of a coffin
Ooo aaa ooo aaa
I opened a door and I saw a skeleton
Ooo aaa ooo aaa.

Shehzad Ahmed (12)

THE CHILLERS

A vampire rose through the coffin
Ooo aaa ooo aaa
A ghost floated above the coffin
Ooo aaa ooo aaa
A dead body stunk of rotten flesh
Ooo aaa ooo aaa
A rat ate the dead body
Ooo aaa ooo aaa
Dracula was hanging by his neck
Ooo aaa ooo aaa
The skeleton rattled his bones
Ooo aaa ooo aaa
A ghost floated above the ground
Ooo aaa ooo aaa
Dead bodies hung from the ceiling
Ooo aaa ooo aaa.

Dale Doherty & Matthew Hayes (12)

MIDNIGHT WANTED

A ghost lived in a lamp post
Ooo aaa ooo aaa
Zombies who lived in old man Gomelis
Ooo aaa ooo aaa
Bats who lived in a black hat
Ooo aaa ooo aaa
Vampires who lurked around at night
Ooo aaa ooo aaa.

Paul Hilton (12)

Mice!

Mice are annoying vermin,
Who go away and keep returning.
They sneak around looking for food
And when they do they're really rude.
They especially hunt around for cheese,
Crawling up legs and people's knees.
They also crawl on the cooks' ladles,
Waking up babies in their cradles.

Kirsty Tarkenter (13)

MICE

They're little and furry,
Their tails are pink,
Their faces are hairy,
They're not very scary.

They eat all the cheese,
Which makes you quease,
They live in the gutters,
Which gives me the flutters.

Some are brown,
Others are white,
Some are black,
As black as night.

They scurry and hurry,
Around the floor,
Looking for food,
Old pieces that we've already chewed.

Chelsea Battersby (12)

Poem About Vermin

Snakes and rats,
Frogs and bats,
These are what I hate most.

Slugs and snails,
Poor puppy dogs' tails,
With jam all spread on toast.

A dog and a cat,
A Guinea pig and all that,
I love them most.

A goldfish,
In a dish,
But not with jam and toast!

Danielle Jardine (12)

BATS

Bats, bats, bats,
They don't look like cats
Like the moon ain't made out of cheese
And that will put your mind at ease.

They're hairy, they're scary
They're fast and black
And never get a sore back
They shout and screech
Like they're saying a speech
And they're also out of their mind.

They're horrible, they're terrible
They turn you black and blue
They also make you laugh too
But then it makes you need the loo.

Samantha Harper (12)

Pigeons

There was once a town called Oldham,
Which was infested by vermin
The vermin was pigeon
And they were even in your kitchen!

The pigeons got everywhere
Even in your underwear!
They pinched and scratched and ate and ate
They even nibbled at your gate!

The pigeons were such a menace
They went in your purse and nicked your pennies
By the time you had shooed them out
You had to shout and shout and shout.

Melanie Thomas (12)

RATS!

Rats, rats I hate rats,
they live inside,
stinky old hats.
The cats kill the rats
and the rats kill the cats.
When they bite you,
you die, I can't tell a lie,
everybody hates *rats!*

Daniel Stacey (12)

A Poem About Pigeons

Pigeons are smelly,
they have big fat bellies.
They have wings and feathers
and they eat rubbish.

Pigeons are smelly,
they have big fat bellies.
They flap and flutter
and poo on people's heads.

Pigeons are smelly,
they have big fat bellies.
They sit on fences,
if they're too fat they fall off.

Andrew Hurst (12)

RATS

The big black rats are ugly and fat,
They're slimy and grimy and terrible, blimey,
They make people cry they're hairy and scary,
Rats, rats, rats, rats,
They have black diamond eyes
That look like the skies,
They look like ugly dogs and are little blobs.

They're invading the shops and breaking the cheese pots,
They're fighting the dogs and chasing the cats,
They're scaring the town and eating around.

Then along came Jamie,
Cheese on his left and pellet gun on his right,
Bang, bang, bang all the rats were down.

Dean Barry (12)

NETBALL

The players are strong the players are tough
the players are very very rough.
They pass the ball here and there
they pass it everywhere.
The players move up and down
side to side and all around,
it starts to rain
oh no I am getting wet
I can see everybody running but not my pet.
He likes the rain
he is mad
I think he is sad.
It's time to go now
but I had a great day
now I will say
bye bye, hooray!

Sheree Naylor (12)

THE MILLENNIUM

As we approach the millennium
There will be such a lot to do
Like sorting out computers and electricity too
We really don't know what to expect
In the year 2000 ahead
There will be such a lot of surprises
It will include everybody and me.

Leigh Robinson (12)

The Year 2000

Two thousand years have just passed by
A new time has begun
To have a laugh and drink some beer
To party and have fun
I'm looking forward to this night
When people in each town
Are waiting very anxiously for
One clock to count down
I don't know what will happen
It will be a surprise
But fireworks will light the sky
And light up people's eyes
The millennium is nearly here
It's time to look behind
The millennium is a new start of a century
And a new start for mankind.

Christina Marshall (12)

My Dog Sam

It was a lovely summer's day, I lay down on the grass,
I saw a hawk soar to the sky and butterflies fly past.
The bees were buzzing, the river rippled, it made me fall asleep.
I had a dream, I went to Heaven and saw my old dog Sam.
We used to call him Sam the man for he was more than human.
He was a dear old friend to me, I loved him so very much.
I wish that I could bring him back but I am quite content,
Because I know the dream I had was surely heaven sent.

Sean Mooney (12)

My Dog Max

My dog Max is really funny
because when you throw a stick
he chases my brother.
When you say 'play dead'
he runs in the kitchen
and looks for a very sharp knife.
When you say roll over
he rolls all over my gran
and starts licking.
I love my dog Max
because he makes me laugh
when you say do something funny.

Martin Kuhnert (13)

SEASONS OF THE YEAR

Spring
New life begins,
Trees come into leaf and bud,
Yellow daffodils gently sway in the breeze,
Crocuses and tulips show a blaze of colour,
The world awakes - spring is here.

Summer
School's out - hurray!
Long hot sunny days are here,
Children are water fighting, skipping,
Throwing balls on dusty streets,
Exotic holidays are enjoyed by those fortunate enough
To travel to far off lands,
Others go to seaside destinations nearer to home,
The world is happy - summer is here.

Autumn
Leaves fall, flowers die,
Trees become bare, piles of leaves rustle on the ground,
Scenery changes colour from the bright hues of summer
To the russet shades now seen,
Birds migrate, animals hibernate,
Screeching Catherine wheels, whooshing rockets hurtling skywards
Are heard in the November air,
The world celebrates bonfire night - autumn is here.

Winter
Snowflakes fall,
Footprints are seen in the crispy white snow,
People shiver with the cold weather outside
And huddle around the fire indoors,
Their hunched bodies can be seen as they rush home from work,
Fighting the harsh elements,
Suddenly happy faces can be seen.

Bright lights decorate the streets, Christmas is coming,
People shop for presents, turkeys and mince pies,
Jesus' birth is celebrated by many far and wide in different ways,
Children rush downstairs to open their presents on Christmas morning -
Their faces shining with excitement,
The world is at peace - winter is here.

Shaista Bano (12)

AUTUMN

A utumn
U nder the
T rees lay the leaves
U nder the ground, squirrels
M uck about
N ibbling nuts and laughing about.

Rachel Lomas (11)

Millennium Words

Words have been with us since the beginning of time;
I was told that when you write a poem,
you should write things that come straight out of your mind,
to sit and think . . .

like a new dawn, a new era.
Like Shakespeare wrote,
'Who is it, that can tell me
who I am?'
Or, 'Is that a blue cloud or
am I just dreaming?'
It makes you think doesn't it?
A wondrous philosophy to evoke.
It is an enigmatic sight to see,
the dawn of the millennium.
Like night is vanquished,
almost as if it is judgement day.
December 31st 1999,
everyone will celebrate it with exaltation.
It is a spectacular evolution,
a feral time, which will seem only
to last a few minutes.

Nell Cook (12)

My Best Friend

My best friend is important to me,
I am very lucky to have a great best friend.
When something is lost it is being found.
Only one true friend can help me
And that is my best friend.
We meet in school and sometimes the library.
She is always there to help,
My best friend is there when I need her.
Sometimes she plays jokes on me and says funny things.
I never say bad things about her because I know
My friendship is something to earn.
We always hang around at breaks and afternoons.
We always listen to each other.
My best friend always cheers me up when I'm sad.
Long life to her. We will be best friends forever
And know each other for years and years.
Sometimes we break up but we make up at the end.
That's how it will always be forever and ever.
No one can take the place of my best friend.

Resma Khatun (12)

Bonfire Night

The 5th of November smells of burning wood.
Fireworks light up the night sky.
Children's faces light up watching the fireworks
swirl and whizz in the sky.
Dogs howling at all the fizzes and whizzes outside.
A lovely sweet smell of trickly toffee and toffee apples.
Sparklers fizzing, looking like stars.
Rockets go blasting off with a loud screech.
Guy Fawkes burning on the blazing hot yellow flames.
The day after bonfire night there's still a smell of burning wood
leftover, toffee apple, last remains of the rockets
and you can still see your Guy Fawkes burnt to the crisp
until next November 5th.

Kelly Hadaway (12)

My Pony

I dream of owning my own pony
I would like to have a chestnut mare
I would name my pony Chelsea
She would have a sleek body and long legs
So she could run like the wind
She would have a long flowing mane and tail
I would brush her every day to keep her coat shiny.

I would spend all my time looking after my pony
I would feed her morning and night
I would exercise her every day
I would look after her when she is sick
I would play with her when she is looking for fun
I would clean her stable and give her fresh straw
I would give her clean water to drink.

My pony would have a large field to run in
She would have a lovely stable to sleep in at night
I would clean her saddle and bridle so it does not go old
I would cover her with a blanket when it is cold
My pony and I would be best friends
I would whisper to her all my secrets
When I put her to bed I would kiss her goodnight.

Oh how I wish I could have a pony
If I could have a pony I would be nice every day
I would help out with all the chores around the house
Maybe I could put it on my Christmas list
I wonder if I will get one gift-wrapped under the Christmas tree
Or maybe I will just have to spend each day dreaming I have a pony
Whatever happens I will carry on dreaming about my pony
Chelsea.

Katrina O'Brien (12)

THE BURNING OF THE LEAVES

Now is the time for the burning of the leaves.
They go on the fire;
the nostrils prick with smoke
wandering slowly into a weeping mist.
Brittled and blotched, ragged and rotten sheaves!
A flame seizes the smouldering ruin
and bites on stubble stalks that crackle as they resist.

Stuart Mills (12)

OLDHAM GIRL

I'm an Oldham lassie
And I think I'm very classy
My mum never disagrees
She says I'm the bee's knees.
I've got a little sister
Who I call my skin and blister
I'm always happy
And very rarely snappy.
In the week I go to school
To stop me in the future being a fool.
I like playing out
I'm always about.
I ride my bike
To Hartshead Pike
I have friends aplenty
Round about twenty.
We like to go shopping
Sometimes go bopping.
I think now I'll have to stop
Because my mum wants me to go to the shop
It's time for tea you see
For my little sister and me.

Danielle Tracey (12)

My Hero

I wandered lonely down the street,
As I saw a pair of feet,
I looked up and saw his face glowing,
Then I realised it was Michael Owen
My hero.

I walked on
Then looked around
And in despair
The vision I saw
Was no longer there
Michael Owen
My hero.

Angela Marriott (12)

SUMMERTIME

Summertime's a great time I know
Umbrellas down, away with the snow
Most people say that summers are too hot
But I say the opposite, summers are top.
The sun in the sky, the sea so calm
People lie on the seashore
Soaking up the sun, which we adore
That is why the summer's such fun
I love the sun more than anyone.

Gemma Buckley (12)

My Trip To France

It was the first time I was going to France,
But all I wanted to do was dance,
I packed my bags,
Full of rags,
I rang my friend and promised to send a postcard to her house,
I ran out the door,
Kissing goodbye,
And then I thought that I could fly.

When I got there,
I was brushing my hair,
Wondering what it is like over there.

When we arrived,
I just had to dive straight into the pool that was there,
But I was a fool 'cause it was so cool.

Soon we had to go,
Which made me sad,
One reason it made me glad,
To see my mam and dad.

Sarah Holbrook (12)

Wrestling

Wrestling, wrestling I love it so much
With all of those muscly lot.
Giving me entertainment in the ring
And all of the hate it can bring.
Steve Austin and Triple H,
Knocking each other out all over the place,
It is a real big disgrace.
X-Pac and Kane and Road Dog too,
Are the favourites of me and you.
I watch the wrestling every week,
I never miss a single bit.
With Rock and Mankind and Sockhole too,
They never ever want to lose.
Ten o'clock in the morning,
It's the place to be,
Sky Sports 1,
It's great for me!
My dad's favourite is the people's champ *The Rock!*
My brother's favourite is *Triple H!*
Mum says 'What's all the fuss about?
It's only wrestling there's no need to shout!'
We can't make her understand!
It's not for girls,
It's just for boys!
With Chris Jericho who everyone hates
And the Mean Street Posse it's all so great.
Well I think so
It keeps me off the streets!
My tape collection
Is getting very big
That's pretty neat!

Christian Knott (11)

EMILY AND ROCHELLE

Emily and Rochelle are my bestest friends,
They're always there for me.
People often stop and say,
'Here comes the terrible three!'
We laugh and cry and scream and shout
And look out for each other,
Especially when we're trying to hide,
From my little kid brother!

Stacey Woodhead (11)

Who Am I?

I am a human being,
I can do whatever I want.
I write in whatever font.

I am brass champion of the world,
I can have little fear,
I am a princess in the sunshine.

I am a girl who is always fine,
I am whoever I want to be,
But best of all I am me.

Victoria Kenworthy (11)

A Mother's Love

A mother's love is like a rose
Never dies, forever grows
Always in her arms she holds
Her little angel, me.
When I'm ill she cradles me
The amount of love you cannot see
Between my mother and me
A mother's love is like a rose
Never dies, forever grows.

Kerry Kendrick

RUNNING FAST DOWN THE STREET

Running fast
down the street
if you hear
something creak
look again
to be sure
if you're not
slam the door!

Jiten Panchani (12)

DREAM

All I ever do is dream
to be the next English queen.
To marry somebody very rich
I can't imagine life in a ditch.

All I ever do is dream
to maybe one day reach the moon.
To touch the stars and the sun
or maybe, this cannot be done.

All I ever do is dream
to travel the world like a beauty queen.
To go through Egypt and through Spain
and never to wake up again.

All I ever do is dream
maybe I'll be a movie queen.
Leonardo Di Caprio will be in my scene.
Just like the Titanic it would be
but in my dream it would be
him and me.

Helen Warburton (13)

My Millennium Poem

To see the millennium is a once in a lifetime event.
It's free, it's fun, it's exciting and happens every
thousand years.
All you do is raise your glass, wait till midnight
then say *cheers!*
Offer out kisses, make your wishes,
set off fireworks - watch them explode.
Do the *conga* in the middle of the road.
Make a New Year's resolution,
Think about your year's solution,
All the trouble you had last year.
Let your family help keep them near.
Drink yourself stupid - call on Cupid.
New year's romance is very rare,
you could leave the party bare.
I'm going to have to end it here
I have just one thing to say and that is -
Happy New Year.

Rebecca Duggan (12)

The Young Kitten's Day

See the kitten on the wall
snatching the leaves as they fall.
Withered leaves one, two, three
falling from the elder trees.
Through the calm and frosty air
of the morning, bright and fair.

See the kitten, how she starts
crouches, stretches, pause - then darts.
A tiger-leap halfway
then she meets her coming prey.
Lets it go as fast as that
has it in her power again.

See the kitten jumping up
ready to lap her milk up.
After her playful day
she wastes no time to end the day.
Crouched up tight on the pillow,
she soon purrs loudly, happy as glee.

Claire Molden

GROOVE RIDER

The grids are up
engines are running.
Helmets, gloves and body-armour
they're all in line.
Numbers and track are fine.
The flag goes down
the grids drop and they're off.
Dust flies everywhere at the bend
noise grows distance
running, running.
Now they're on the eighth
level at the table top.
Passing on the bend.
Flying over jumps,
pipping at the post.
To be number one, of course.

Paul Stevenson (12)

THE MILLENNIUM

The millennium is ten minutes near
My dad's already had ten pints of beer.
We talk about people we love dear
Who are no longer around to see the millennium year.

The millennium is five minutes near,
Our family and friends gather round to cheer.
They joke and laugh and drink more beer
And hope their dreams come true this year.

The clock strikes twelve - aliens appear!
Blast-guns in their pockets - big pointed ears.
I'm told to get into their ship - they're taking me on a special trip,
Shooting around the stars - they even took me to Mars!

Now it's time for them to rule,
No more teachers, nor more school.
The aliens are cool, so there's nothing to fear,
Happy New Year! The millennium's here!

Thomas MacNeill (12)

Sport

Sport keeps us all fit
Every sport has a different bit.

Every game has different rules
A stadium to play at or swimming pools.

Always do warm-ups before the game
Unless you want your muscles to be in a lot of pain.

The score always counts at the end of the game
Because before you know it, your name is in fame.

It's time for a shower after the game
Everyone's sweating, they all look the same.

Back at home, it's time for a rest,
This time next week I'll beat the best.

Adam Pratt (12)

THE COUNTDOWN

Ten, nine, eight, seven - every day, every second
counting down to the millennium.
Ninety-eight days to the big celebration
at the end of century.

People say - remember the good old days?
But the youth of today don't want to look back
to the bleak old days.
The new century is more up their way.

Kirsty Roberts (12)

My Millennium Wish

The new millennium is going
to be cool.
I know exactly what I'm
going to do.
I'll start by playing football
for Liverpool,
And of course dating
Michael Owen.
I'll live in Disneyland
and never go to school.
We'll dance all day and
scream and shout.
On the big, big roundabout.
It's going to be fun, it's
going to be great
because I'm on a date.

Jenna Sowerby (12)

THE FUTURE

The future is here right now
This very day, hour, minute and second
Every second gone is the past
Every second to come is the future.

How the future develops is up to us
We as teenagers, we the new generation
We are the future, we will advance,
We will change and improve technology.

But we also have a responsibility
A huge responsibility to this planet
Is our future limited - due to our destruction?
We will have no future unless we stop the damage.

Every second of every day our world
Is being destroyed by pollution
By planes, cars and unrecycled rubbish
If the world continues this way
Will we have a future?

Gemma Gregory (13)

I Don't Know What To Wear!

'I don't know what to wear!'
'How about your new blue dress?'
'No, everyone will stare.'
'How about your flares?'
'They go nice with your hat.'
'No, my flares make me look fat.'
'Your pink dress?
That always looks nice.'
'It makes me look like Baby Spice'
'Aha! I've got it.
Your long black skirt.'
'People will think I'm a flirt.
I want something short.
I've thought and thought,
My new blue dress!'
'Ow! Yes! Yes!'

Carley Gartland (11)

SNOW!

The crisp white snow falls silently to the ground
It doesn't make a single sound.
We have to wrap up really warm
Especially at early morn.
You look outside, it's really white
Everywhere you looked, it's in your sight.
It's really good when you play out
It's only because you're allowed to shout.
You can build snowmen as big as you like
But you can't ride your bike.
You never see butterflies or things like that
But you always have to wear a bobbly hat.
You see the footprints in the snow
Crunch, crunch, crunch - there they go.
It's getting dark now, nearly night
But the snow is sparkling and bright.
Sun is shining, nice and light
Snow is melting, what a sight.

Catherine Barran (11)

TELEVISION

T elevision is great
E ven when you have the flu it always gives you something to do
L ucky people like me have Sky
E very night I watch Time Go By
V ideos are okay
I nteresting films you can watch
S aturday night at ten is a lot
I can watch it anywhere
O n and on and on
N ow it's time for this to end and have yourself a nice weekend.

Claire Marrow (11)

COLOURS

Orange:
Orange is the colour of an orange, juicy and sweet
Orange is the sand, hot under your feet.
Orange is the ball I like to kick
Orange is the colour I wanted to pick.

Black:
Black is the sky at night
Black is the coal not at all bright
Black is my friend's mountain bike
Black am I when I go on a hike.

Green:
Green is the grass so short
Green is the lizard that I once bought
Green are the leaves in spring
Green is the cloak owned by the king.

Red:
Red is a toffee, sour and sweet
Red is the coat warn by me
Red is the tomato in my tea
Red is the leaves off a tree.

Blue:
Blue is the sky high above me
Blue is the dolphin swimming in the sea
Blue is the colour of my new car bumper
Blue is the colour of my old school jumper.

Grey:
Grey is the colour of any bats wing
Grey is the rock in my mum's ring
Grey is the colour of any large elephant
Grey is the colour of my school pants.

Lee T Hughes (12)

MILLENNIUM

What will it be like?
Will the world end?
Will we start to live with aliens
Or will we start to ride in spaceships?
All these questions are going through my mind.
Does anybody know what it will be like?
People say we will lose all of the lights and
All of the computers will shut down.
Maybe the world will change.
Will it be good or will it be bad?
Nobody knows the answers
So I guess we'll have to wait and see
What the millennium is all about.

Sarah Mellor (13)

Colours

Red, white, yellow and blue
These are the colours that remind me of you.
Red for love
White for hate
Yellow for kindness
And blue for true.
These are the colours that remind me of you.

Amanda Seville (11)

THE LION

The lion is a ferocious beast
His teeth can make anyone his feast.
Those fangs, which are as sharp as the
horns of a bull.
They make him powerful.
Those muscular legs give him his speed,
The animals he sees he thinks he must lead.

Vincent Barton (11)

UNDER THE SEA

Under the sea I
like to go,
and watch all the fish
swim and grow.
There're dolphins and
sharks, stingrays too.
They eat and sleep just
like we do.
Fish come in lots of
sizes and colours, they
have lots of sisters and
lots of brothers.
My favourite fish is the
Flounder, it puffs out
fat then goes smaller.
They come in many
colours mostly orange
and white.
The white is very dark
and the orange is very
bright.
The dolphin is blue and a
mammal like me and you.
And that's why I would like
to visit the deep, deep
blue sea.

Estelle Beckett (11)

THIS POEM IS ABOUT ME

This poem is about me
My name is Emma Lee.
I love my dog (she's a chow chow)
And I know my dog loves me.
I go to school and follow the rules
Because it's the right thing to do.
I do my work, I do not shirk
I enjoy my playtimes too.
I want to join the orchestra
I'd like to play the flute.
My knowledge of music is basic
But I want to learn (toot, toot).
And pottery I'm interested in,
Although I've never tried,
Unless you count the plasticine doll
I made when I was five.
I've only looked in the art room
It looks quite exciting in there.
I wonder if I'll be clever enough
To display my paintings - but where?
They may end up in the bin, who knows!
When I come home from school at night,
(I'm allowed on my own on the bus).
My mum says I'm old enough now,
So she doesn't make too much fuss.

Emma Kenyon (11)

FOOTBALL

I play football every day
I run around and play,
but when I score
I cheer and roar.
United are the best.

We play on a Sunday
at home or away.
The linesman with his flag,
the trainer with his bag.
United are the best.

It's the start of the match
0 - 0 from scratch,
the whistle blows
and away we go.
United are the best.

Half-time arrives
and there's been some dives
we're winning 2 - 1
can we hang on?
United are the best.

The final whistle goes
the referee blows.
How did the game finish up?
We won the cup!
United are the best.

Mark Davenport (11)

ELEPHANT'S FEATURES

Elephants are big and strong
They have a trunk which is quite long.
Sometimes they have tusks on either side
And they can take people for a ride.

Elephants like to be one of a crowd
They make a noise which is very loud.
They like to have apples for a snack
And roll in the mud and get quite black.

Elephants need our protection
They need our love and affection.
Do not hurt these magnificent creatures
They have so many wonderful features.

Simon Baker (11)

Big School!

'Get up now, it's almost eight.
You said you didn't want to be late.'
'Oh mum! I feel sick!'
'Don't be silly, just be quick!'

Climbed out of bed, dressed myself,
Grabbed my pencil case off the shelf.
Ate some toast, drank some tea
Then my friend Jane, called for me.

We walked to the gates filled with dread.
How I wished I stayed in bed.
All the other pupils look so grown up,
What will we do if we get split up?

The hall seemed full of wriggly worms
The separated - sent to forms.
Split up from friends, sat with a stranger
Filled with fear, even though there's no danger.

Before I know it the lunchtime bell
In the rush I nearly fell.
Ate a pizza, drank some Coke
Saw the *big boys* having a crafty smoke.

Then it's French with Madame Quinn
Learn new words like, '*tres bien'*
My once empty bag is full of books
Time to go home, I turn to look.

My first day at big school over and done
I enjoyed it really, it was fun.
Tomorrow is another day
But for now I'll just go out to play.
. . . 'Rachel! Do your homework!'

Rachel Buckley (11)

FOOD!

Mmm food, yummy food,
Jelly for my enormous belly.

Mmm food, yummy food,
Ice-cream is a dream.

Mmm food, yummy food,
Pork pies for my anxious eyes.

Mmm food, yummy food,
Chocolate cake . . . I feel sick!
Bbbbbllllggghhhh!

Arron Tierney (11)

INSIDE A CHILD'S HEAD!

If I were a bird I would fly so high,
I'd travel the world and visit Dunguy.
Where the whistle trees blow bubbles
from their heads.
The new colour of birds turned out
to be reds!
I would stop for tea in a town called
Mungru,
If you want to come you're very
welcome too!
I would take a drink of the most sour milk
I would also touch a piece of the finest silk.
I'd use my wings to fly up to the stars,
I'd tour the moon, Saturn and Mars.
I'd go in search for a castle on the hills,
I'd track down that monster that
frightens the girls.
Only all my dreams belong in my head,
As my great grandmother has always said.

Hayley Jayne Keight (11)

MONEY

Money is great, it buys lots of good things,
Like shining Ferraris and big diamond rings.
Money is great, it brings me such joy
I can afford new clothes and the latest toy.
I love having money it makes me high,
It makes me so high, I could touch the sky.
If I had pots of money I'd go on a big shopping trip,
Then I'd travel round the world on a big sailing ship.
I hate it when I've got absolutely none,
I can't buy new things - 'cause all the money's gone!

Katy Bailey (11)

The Monster

I was asleep in my bed, with nice dreams spinning through my head
When instantly
I felt a chill, so I went downstairs to get a drink of milk.
And suddenly I heard a noise, at first I thought it was one of my toys,
So I started looking wary, then I saw something small, furry and scary.
Then I felt something on my foot, it looked like it was covered in soot,
I ran indoors, locking front and back doors,
I ran to my bed, terrible thoughts racing through my head.
After a while, I felt okay, I hoped the monster had gone away.
Then my door gave a creak and I heard a small squeak
I got under my covers, how I wished I was asleep.
I know I'll take a look, a little peep,
I wonder what it is?
The thing was over by the door, what it was, I wasn't sure.
I walked over to my mat, and there it was.
Why I'd been scared I don't know,
Because sat on my mat was a little black
harmless . . . cat.

Kieran Platt (11)

Cars

Subaru have the engines
Porsche have the looks
Good luck in buying one because
They cost too much.

Vauxhall are cheap
Compared to some cars
But if you get in a Mini
You've gone too far.

Jaguar are classics
Mercedes too
But the only problem is
At the moment they cost too much
For you and me.

BMW is the car my dad wants to own
And maybe someday he will have one of his own.

Ferrari are smart cars they're one of the best
And when I get a little bit older who knows
I may put one to the test.

Mitsubishi is a sports car which looks really cool
But when I get rich I would like one parked
Next to my pool.

Honda NSX - RGT is a dream
That when you drive it on the road
It will make you scream.

Nissan Skyline is one of the best in its class
You're very lucky if you see it all
All because it's very fast.

Liam Lyons (11)

FEARS

Fears show your weaknesses
even if you don't show them,
and if it is not noticed in the naked eye.

You can be fearful of anything
and they usually hit the soft spot.

A fear such as of spiders can be avoided
you can bottle it up.
Scream when no one's there.

But a fear of love is quite different,
you're scared of loving someone,
as they may not experience any love for you.

An even bigger fear is when
your fears eventually take you over.

And when they fall in love
with another person other than you.

It becomes a fear when you
haven't experience it and it slowly
creeps up on you.
Just like a spider!

Andrea Peel (16)

Breaking Of A Nation's Heart

In World War II
Children were sent away.
Sixty years later
They made a play.
The children - one five, the other six
Played the part
Filled with sadness and fear.
They portrayed the feelings that they had
And with it came a tear.
As the grandparent's remembered
That same old lonesome year.
They remembered their *fosters*
The few cold-hearted
And the others - kind.
Others told about the Victorian-minded *fosters*
Who made you clean the house
And eat - standing up in silence,
So quiet you could hear a mouse.
They were so homesick
They missed their families.
One child was moved three times
Before a home he found.
His mother's words:
'Don't worry,
It won't be too long now,
The war will end for good and soon we'll all be free.'
Who knew how wrong she'd be?
His wife, who left too
Told of how it didn't bother her
How strong children were then!
The posters on the walls
Show the pressure on the parents.
Of Hitler whispering to a mother:
'Take them back. Take them back. Take them back!'
'Leave them where they are' they said.
'They're safe where they are!'

Safely out of the way.
Some were sent to the countryside.
Where the animals graze and crops grow.
There they saw the springtime,
And the flowers they did sow.
So in short, this story's moral is
The war was long and sad for us all,
But the breaking of a nation's heart
Was the saddest of them all.

Nicola Ford (13)

PRIMARY SCHOOL TERRORS

Barry and I
Primary School terrors.

What did we do?
Nothing much!
Only throwing wet bog roll
at the girls!
The worst thing,
The funniest thing,
The baddest thing was when we
got Paul Glue.

What did we do?
Nothing much!
Only pushed him into a hook
only Paul Glue.

'Oh, the blood, oh the gore!'
Barry said. 'I can see his brain.'
I said 'Does he have one?'

Mathew Mosoph (14)

MEMORIES POEM

I was on my cousin's wall.
That's what I like to do
sitting
and chatting
and as we were chatting
my friend's little brown dog
came over
and jumped on me.
What should I do?
Falling back - I trapped my finger.
Crying and screaming
and then taking me to hospital.
I said 'No! They're going to do an operation.'
They said 'No!'
The nurse cleaning,
putting medicine and a plaster on.
I was very good.
I got a certificate.

Sameena Bibi (14)

St George's Square Nursery

Me and Matty
met
in the nursery.
Matty's a cheeky
little boy.

We played
we laughed
we messed about
in the nursery.

We messed about
in Primary School.
You'd never believe it.
Here's what we did.

Flicked elastic bands
had food fights.
Went into the classrooms
flooded the toilets
and the sinks.

I've not been
naughty in
Secondary School yet!
Matt has!

Barry Woodhouse (14)

MEMORIES POEM

I mean
It's not the first time
Or the second
Or the third
Or fourth
Or fifth
Probably the sixth time
I've been in hospital.

Jamie said,
'Let's race round the block.'
My stomach was full of
Chicken soup and chicken butties.

We started racing
I ran round the corner and fell.
I smashed my hand on a milk bottle,
Blood flooded from my wound.

It was on my top
On my pants
On my watch
And all over my arms and face.

I went to hospital
I had an operation.
I stayed in over night
I was allowed to go home.

Robin Garside (14)

Little Laura Kane

Little Laura Kane was going to play with friends,
But she didn't come home.
No sign of Laura anywhere
A nine year old in the dark alone.

Where could she be on this stormy night?
A police search was announced.
Looking in forests and woods
Asking house to house.

Ten days had passed and nothing was heard,
Looking here, looking there.
Where could she be?
No sign of Laura anywhere.

Mr Bainbridge was working at Laura's home the day she disappeared,
Laura was found in his house, sadly not alive.
Under floorboards - Colin had tried to hide,
The body of a child named Laura Kane.

How could somebody do that to a child?
Colin had a child of his own.
He must have felt the guilt,
Killing a child that had barely grown.

Laura will never graduate, or buy a home,
Get married or have a child of her own.
To imagine the pain, he has caused brings a tear to my eye,
Because a young child should never deserve to die.

Claire Dowey (13)

The Crash

Eleven people boarded the Cessna 404
Eight of them didn't know they would never
come back again.
As I was having a tea-break, after hours of
hard work - landscaping.
I saw a plane flying low and plummeting
nose first.
Then it crashed.
The plane hit the ground.
I heard screaming
I rushed to the plane
but the heat was too intense, like the sun.
I thought of nothing except to help the people screaming.
Boom! Boom!
Explosions erupted and then I heard the engine splutter.
I figured out one of the engines had gone down,
because of the way it swooped right,
like a bird in flight.
My hand was shaking
I was so nervous.
The plane was in three parts
blazing away.
Dying victims were screaming.
The emergency services arrived.
I told them what had happened and I stayed and helped.
I will never forget the day of the crash of a Cessna 404.

Stewart Maxwell (13)

THE BIG TOP BELSEN

We walked to the Belsen of Big Tops not knowing
what to expect.
'Why don't you go to the Belsen of Big Tops?' someone said.
We took their advice and now regret it

We were very excited before the show
Until the performers and animals came out.
We were shocked at the way the poor animals were treated.

The bears were the worst
They had young cubs that had been taken away
Locked up in a cramped cage for twenty-three hours a day

Imagine how it must feel to see your mother
for just an hour a day
Their cries for their mothers were so sad
We asked a police officer to stop this cruelty
They just shrugged their shoulders and told us
'There is nothing we can do.'

Then the lions and tigers entered the circus ring
The animals were barely moving and all you could see
Were the artists trying to make the best out
of their ability to perform

By now we couldn't bear to watch anymore of the performances
We demanded to see the manager at once
And wouldn't leave until he arrived

The manager came and told us to leave
He said 'The circus has a licence to use animals.'
He denied that the circus abused and forced the
animals to perform

We left the circus at once and at the back of the tent
We saw a man forcing a tiger up a ramp leading
to the circus ring

We decided that we weren't going to see any more of this
We could only hope that the animals would pull through
this torture
And still be alive to be set free from the circus.

Selina Sin (14)

I Was A Joyrider

It was on a Wednesday evening
a few years ago in March.
Me and my friend Emma
helped to nick a car.

We went around to the Estate,
and found one we could take.
The lads got in and hot-wired it,
the engine was awake.

I strapped myself in safely
and held onto the sides.
I didn't know it was to be
a roller-coaster ride.

We pulled out of an alley
and onto the main street.
The car was swerving wildly,
I was slipping down my seat.

I suddenly felt quite nauseous
and I wanted to get out.
But the adrenaline kept me going
though I started to have doubts.

The excitement was amazing
and the atmosphere was tense.
I started to relax a bit
but then I saw the fence . . .

Amy Carter (13)

My Girls

Tiegan you don't know how much you
mean to me,
One special girl is all I can
see,
You are healthy and you are
bright,
To me you are the most
beautiful sight.

When you are older you will
understand,
That you have completed
my demand.
My unhealthy baby deserved
a better life,
In Heaven she lives on, as my
sweet Serena.

Sweet Serena it was for the
best,
I now understand you have left
my nest,
The river has flowed and left
me behind
But it has taken you Serena
to a whole new world.

I have an aim in life for my
baby girl,
To protect my Tiegan like
an ancient pearl.
Serena, you I will never forget,
Tiegan and Serena if only
had met.

Jodie Byrne (13)

A SHORT LIFE

The mud's up to my calves
The wind tousles my hair,
But my family's inside
Warm and without a care.

While just around the corner
A mum's joy will turn to sorrow,
When her newly born baby
Will not live to see tomorrow.

She'd gone through all the hard stuff,
Like giving birth to her little boy,
But the things that should come after
She will not get to enjoy.

The death sentence fell
When he was born male,
Though he's healthy and fit
From his head down to his tail.

I walked to the field
And opened the gate,
Then started to lead him
To his dreadful fate.

He clip-clopped through the courtyard
A little trusting soul,
He stopped to have a last drink
From a battered metal bowl.

Now comes the bit
Which we farmer's hate,
I unhinged the catch
On the old squeaky gate.

I took him inside
The old wooden barn,
And then tied him up
With a short piece of yarn.

A man lined the gun
With the little calf's head
I closed my eyes
Then bang! He was dead!

If it wasn't for the Government
And the market crash.
The calves could keep living
Drinking milk and eating grass.

Jessica Rigby (13)